THE PRODIGAL THE PROCLAMATION & THE PROPHETIC

WILLIAM OKYERE

For details about other books by the author and
speaking engagements,
please contact him on +233 557 581 505
email: pneumeduf@yahoo.com

ISBN: 978-9988-2-9643-8

Printed and Published by
Pastor William Okyere
Tel: 233 55 758 1505
pneumeduf@yahoo.com

We are born to embark on a journey -
from an earthly father to a heavenly One

William Okyere

ACKNOWLEDGMENT

This book has become a reality by the encouragement of many, especially members of the Stripes of Jesus Alumni and House of Judah social media platforms, and also members of IBC-Dakar, who made time to read my postings. Your feedback assured me that the materials were worth reading. I say thank you. And a special one to Apostle Samuel Lartey and Uncle Brian Sapati; your comments were very encouraging. You strengthened my desire to write more. A very big thank you.

Proof reading, formatting and laying out the text and pre-press design would have been daunting without the selfless assistance of Pastor Samuel Colley. I say thank you. Additional help was also provided by my student, Mayor W. M. Narh of Victory International Bible Training School, Tema. My appreciation also to Mr. Daniel Asare and Mr. Gnonsio Arthur, all of Manna Mission, for further suggestions. I am however responsible for the contents of this book. I apologize for any part of this book that may "offend" any reader. That is not my intention. I want to say a big thank you to Rev. Dr. Seth Ablorh, President of Manna Mission Inc., Rev. Kwame Owusu Baafi, Senior Pastor of International Baptist Church of Dakar, and Osomfo John Mensah Acquaye, my first bible school principal for the positive influence over my life and ministry. Also to Rev. I.K. Owusu, Senior Pastor of Redeemed Baptist Church, who trusted me with the Evangelism Emphasis Week program that gave birth to this book.

A special thanks to Alice, my wife of twenty eight years, and all my children for the wonderful support they gave while working on this book.

PREFACE

Structuring and formatting the contents of this book did not come easily. It is because this did not start as a book. It started as discussions on the social media platform. It started in a "seed" form as a series of topics for an Evangelism Emphasis Week with Redeemed Baptist Church where I worshiped at the time. Responses from this program, coupled with those I received from social media platforms and churches (including Rhema World Ministries and Greater Grace Outreach Ministry) encouraged me to bind these thoughts into a book. Although the topics for the Evangelism Emphasis Week were all centered on the Parable of the Prodigal Son, I have, in this book, added two series that were also discussed on the social media platform that I had titled as the Superlatives of the Gospel and also the Prophetic in the Church today.

The details of this book therefore come in brief pieces. I realised it was respectful not to overload my social media friends since our platforms are loaded with thousands of other information. I have always believed that the Word of God is like medicine; it must be taken in dosages all through our lifetime. No topic discussed here is exhaustive. However, I believe it will draw the readers' attention to what the Holy Spirit has been saying to us all this while. We do not hear Him because the noise from the other side is distracting our attention.

Seriously, millions are entering into eternity every second without having a close contact with the gospel. I know many believers are concerned about sharing the gospel; their only problem is how to share it and what to say. Some portions of this book can be a starter.

CONTENT

THE PARABLE OF THE PRODIGAL SON

INTRODUCTION

Born in the Ashanti Region, I have always had childhood friends in Kumasi, Ashanti Region's capital. Every visit to Kumasi brought me into contact with someone who knew me as the little boy, affectionately called "Quaycoo", a pet form of Kweku (a Wednesday-born).

One of such fellows, was not just a friend but a brother to me. As children, soccer was our passion. We could make a soccer ball out of anything 'kickable'; from plastic bottles to items that could be molded into anything thing that looked like a ball. But as we grew, we were separated by distance and also by life's choices. I became a pastor and he continued playing soccer. Once a while I visited, and we had the opportunity of playing back pleasant childhood memories.

I had to travel to Kumasi quite regularly and my good friend, was always available to keep me company. On some days he made sure I had enough food to eat. Other times, keeping me company was all I needed.

Whilst everything apparently looked normal in those days, there was a battle raging in my heart any time I visited. There probably was also a battle raging in his heart too. I could not tell about his, but mine was simply a heavy burden to share with my friend the good news of Christ my Savior. Disobediently, I always numbed the urge to witness about Christ but rather assured myself that I will do that another time.

Time went by and characteristically as was our custom, we had a beautiful time laughing together during one of my visits. He was never short of stories. During this visit, he told me of an interesting story about a "burger" (someone who has returned from abroad). This "Burger" had wasted all his resources on women and on a life of debauchery until everything was gone. He now had no food to eat. He had to help a lady preparing one of the cheapest local dishes every morning by running errands, clearing food leftovers and doing dishes. His remuneration for all that labor was a plate of food a day. "Burger" had earned himself a nick-name based on the food he received as his salary for the day. Soon everybody started calling him "burger kokonte". As he shared with me, the burden to share the gospel with him became heavier. I disobeyed and postponed, again; I assured myself saying, "next time I will tell him about Jesus."

Many travel thousands of miles just to meet one soul. How can we be excused if the souls travel to us? My friend came to visit me this time round, and was in no hurry out of our conversation. I had him! I had his heart, I had his time and I had his undivided attention. Did I need a special day earmarked for evangelism?

After a couple of months, I visited my sister and, as usual, had an opportunity to taste a home-made meal. Seeing the food alone was a festival. The anticipation of eating this sumptuous meal heightened the rate at which I was salivating. Just before I could start my meal my sister came close and said to me, "I don't want to forget this. Your friend (name withheld), died", she solemnly said. Shame, guilt, condemnation all poured over me. "God please forgive me. I wish someone shared with him what I had failed to share", I prayed.

On hind sight, my friend had shared with me the Kumasi version of the Parable of the Prodigal Son. I failed to share with him the biblical version of the Parable of the Prodigal Son.

This is one of the many reasons I share this parable with you. May the Holy Spirit throw more light. Blessings.

THE PARABLE OF A FAR COUNTRY   1

It all started with an Evangelism Emphases Week with the Redeemed Baptist Church. All through the program I used the "Parable of the Prodigal Son" in Luke 15:11-32. Because this is the Parable of Parables, the Holy Spirit opened my eyes to understand that each line in the Parable is a parable in itself. So I started with "The Parable of the Far Country" from verses 13-16. Everyone who is not in the Father's House is FAR. The situation may be different from person to person but the fact of remoteness cuts across. But we will not be alarmed with this remoteness until we go a little further with Jesus to the next chapter of Luke 16 where Jesus speaks about the richman and Lazarus. Do not forget that the original bible scripts were not in chapters and verses. The interesting fact about this narrative in Luke 16 is that it is the only in Jesus' teachings where real and historical names are mentioned. Lazarus, Abraham, Moses. What will a real name do for you in hell? So the rich man's name was not mentioned. His name evidently was popular on earth. He had wealth but they had no eternal value.

Is there any link between the Prodigal and this richman? Yes, both of them had wealth. One lost his wealth whilst alive; and the other, at death. The prodigal got hungry but not thirsty but the rich man yearned for only a drop of water. Which means whilst the prodigal was able to return at a certain juncture of his journey, the rich man continued to an unreturnable destination.

The prodigal traveled to a FAR Country, and where the richman was, he could see Abraham and Lazarus AFAR off. (Luke 16:23) *'And beside all this, between us and you there is a great gulf fixed: so that they which would pass from thence to you cannot; neither can they pass to us, that would come from thence."*

IT IS FAR. The living without Christ are FAR but we can help them return home. They are on the highway, traveling very fast. Rescue them whilst they are within reach. Nothing else can be done when the boundary is crossed.

THE PARABLE OF A FAR COUNTRY   2

He had crossed the great gulf, the final destination of all those who pursue the journey to the Far Country without return. The one at the living side on the Far Country said, *'I will arise and go to my Father',* but the one at the dead side, *'That thou (you) wouldest (would) send him to my father's house."* Both of them remembered their father's house; one returned but the other could not because the return journey was not 'travelable'.

You see, I started by stating that this was probably the only narrative Jesus told with real and historical names. Is it possible this rich man lived in the time of Moses or thereabout? (Luke 16:29) If he did, then he has been there for over 3500 years now. In that Far Country, we die longer than we live. Somebody who lived for 60 years has been dead for 700 years now. For 700 years now he has been experiencing what is at the other side of the Far Country. It is true we spend all our energies for the period that would be a past tense very soon and hardly any preparation towards ETERNITY. Though the rich was very far in eternity, there is a strong evangelistic appeal for the dwellers of the earth. *"...send him to my father's house: For I have five brethren; that he may testify unto them, lest they also come into this place of torment."* (Luke 6:27, 28).

I'm tormented
I'm tormented in the flame.
I'm tormented.
I'm tormented in the flame.
Come put your finger in the water
Come and cool my tongue.
For I'm tormented in the flame.

We have left this song only for the Children's Service. We adults need this reminder more. To this appeal Abraham responds: "There is Ama, there is Pastor; there is teacher; there is John; and there (here) you are also."

THE PARABLE OF THE WICKEDNESS OF DECEPTION

"And when he came to himself..." Unfortunately, many never come to themselves. Deception is so strong and the enemy does everything to make us see the fake as the real. Unfortunately, the deceived is never excused. For *'there is a way which seems right unto a man but the end therefore are the ways of death.' (Proverbs 14:12).* The way does not end right because it seemed right. Amazingly, deception starts small and

apparently seems un-harmful but the inherent danger is like the effect of a dynamite. The journey that began with a 'gathering together' ended up in "substance wasted"; extravagance ended with famine; it began with inherited ownership and it ended in slavery; the journey began from where servants had more than enough but ended where husks for swine was a delicacy. The way to destruction never ends until sin is admitted. The prodigal son did not say, "I have been deceived", he said, "I have sinned". He chose to be deceived. He hardened his heart to the truth. Today if you will hear his voice, harden not your hearts. (Hebrews 4:7) "Coming to himself" (Luke 15:17) is an indication that deception grows into strong delusion. In other words, we take ownership of the deception and our conscience is totally seared. We become like the madman that drinks from the gutter unperturbed. Until we come to ourselves in repentance and say, "I have sinned." This is where the sinner meets the Savior; where faith embraces GRACE; and the earth causes heaven to rejoice.

Deception - thrives in our search for comfort.

Deception – can be a pathway for convenience.

Deception offers us easy-to-acquire counterfeits.

And behind it all,

Deception is very CRUEL.

'...Wide is the gate, and broad is the way that leadeth (leads) to destruction, and many there be which go in there at.' (Matthew 7:14).

THE PARABLE OF THE DAY GOD WAS SEEN RUNNING

It was Ama's first day at school. Ama had probably interpreted the outing as a regular visit to the mall until, to her dismay, her mom left her. It was an ordeal until at 2pm when mom's car entered the compound. Ama keenly gazed to see who comes out of the car. It was mom. Ama started running not caring what was on the way until she fell into moms waiting arms. Isaiah once saw God seated on His throne (6:1); Stephen saw Jesus standing at the Father's right hand (Acts 7:56); Bartimaeus' cry made the busy Jesus stand still (Mark 10:49). But when was the last time you saw God run like a child? What makes the whole of Heaven rejoice (Luke 15:7) is that same thing that makes God run? The heart beats the fastest when the body runs. The turning of one sinner's heart causes the heart of the immovable God to beat. If there is one thing that makes God 'emotional', it is the sight of a prodigal son returning home.

'But when he was yet a great way off, his father saw him, and had compassion, and ran, and fell on his neck, and kissed him.' (Luke 15:20). Why was it the father that had to run and not the prodigal? The Savior bears more agony than the lost do. You may have seen an insane person eating from the refuse dump or drinking from the gutter. Between the two of you, who suffers more agony? Maybe you will not be moved. But God does because He is a compassionate God. He loves the world and He gave His only Son for every lost soul. (John3:16). The repentance of every sinner is a reimbursement for the blood of His son. Has your running ever being towards lost souls?

A man condemned to death needed a minister to prepare him for eternity before being hanged. The minister cautioned him about eternity without Christ; that hell was everlasting. "Is what you are telling me true?" he asked. "And do you believe it yourself?" he probed further. The minister responded in the affirmative. "I do not believe you Reverend", he challenged. "Because if I knew and believed what you do, I will run across the world and warn all." What makes you run?

THE PARABLE OF THE FATHER AND HIS AVAILABLE PARTNERS

Some key miracles Jesus performed were not without human assistance. The boy's five loaves and two fishes were actually the beginning of the miracle of the feeding of the five thousand. (John 6:1-13). The disciples also helped in the distribution of the miracle. At the wedding of Cana (John 2:1-11), some people provided the initial raw water that our Lord turned into wine and others distributed it. At the raising of Lazarus from the dead (John 11:1-45), some got so close to remove the stone covering the tomb that contained Lazarus' stinking body. When the miracle eventually happened others had to loosen him from the grave clothes. From my personal experience from blacking-out, there is always a temporary memory loss. Especially the things that immediately happened before the unfortunate incidence. So I can imagine Lazarus asking the one removing the grave's clothes from his face the following: "Ah, why is my body and face bound with clothes, and why am I here; where are Mary and Martha? Please tell me what is going on." And this person might have responded, saying: "Lazarus, you died. Your friend Jesus came to raise you up from the dead. Everyone is here and you will see them all very soon." Of course such experiences happen many times at the hospitals too. Do you realize that Jesus' face might not be the first Lazarus saw? Would you also agree that as long as Lazarus gave his testimony, he probably mentioned other names before mentioning Jesus'? We are the human faces of every miracle God performs on earth. The recipients of such miracles may see us before they see God. In fact we would have to redirect them to Jesus and eventually lay the glory where it belongs. It is all because we are His partners. We are laborers together with God... (1Corinthians 3:9).

◼ THE PARABLE OF THE FATHER AND HIS AVAILABLE PARTNERS   2

...the Father said to the SERVANTS, *'Bring forth the best robe, and put it on him; and put a ring on his hand, and shoes on his feet."*

Someone else could have done these better; the elder brother. But he was not available. It initially looks as if he was not available by distance but as the story continues, we realize he was not available in heart also. Distances from our heart's point of view are far longer than the geographical. The prodigal was his only brother. They had played together as children; eaten together all their life; they had shared the same room and done many things together. He had also been in his father's house all this while the prodigal had been away. But when both father and prodigal son needed him in this heart moving experience, he was neither available in heart, nor in person. The father however had the SERVANTS. These servants may not have the experience but they at least had a "servant's heart" to obey without questioning. They may need to come over and over again to ask for the exact location of the beautification items because they may not have known the father's secret places like the elder son. They were the only ones the father had available at that moment. I have been in a bus where the preacher said very heretical things about Jesus. Yet, the Rev. Dr. sat in the same bus listening to the preacher say "Jesus sinned" instead of saying, "He was made to be sin for us". Such a preacher is among many others who are available to be used in the Kingdom.

And you see, the father did the most energy demanding part (the running) and left the most "Thank-You-attracting" parts for his partners to do. The prodigal says "Thank you" to the servant-in-charge of the robes. Repeats same to the one in charge of the shoes. And does the final one to the one in charge of the ring before finally saying the all-rounder "THANK YOU" to the father.

All this while the most qualified was standing outside, complaining about position, demanding appreciation from this GRACIOUS Father and stigmatizing the prodigal. Behold He Comes...

We need not get stuck in non-essentials.

THE PARABLE OF THE LONG- AWAITED PARTY

The Presence That Brought The Party

One gloomy morning a father started looking out of his house because a son he so dearly loved had walked out of his house. Although the eyes and the feet are far apart, they seem to be the closest. For where the eyes see, the feet walk towards. In the "Parable of the Lost Sheep" (Luke 15:3-7), the shepherd left the 99 and went after the one lost sheep. So from the day man sinned, there is a particular presence of God that habitually lives on the 'missions' field. This kind of presence is only experienced by members of the family when He escorts the prodigal son home. There is a presence that comes in worship; there is a presence that comes in prayer, there is a presence that comes at the delivering of the word. But there is a particular presence that comes only when the prodigal son is escorted back home by the father. This we can call the PARTY presence. From the day the son left, there was a particular presence of the father that lived outside the home. The father's cheerful countenance, the father's exuberance was out there searching for the lost; the father's vision was focusing thousands of miles away. So when He commands us to go to the end of the world (Matthew 28:19, 20), he does not say, "I WILL be with you", rather He says, "I AM with you". There is the presence of God that will not leave the "missions field" until the last sinner is won. When the father saw his son a great way (afar) off, he run the whole distance until the father and the son embraced. That run covered the distance between the Kingdom and where the last sinner on earth is situated. There is therefore no situation on earth where you will witness to a sinner that the presence of God will be lacking. He is there; even under the most difficult circumstances. In fact, by running to the prodigal, that great distance away from home, our God takes the kingdom to where the sinner is - The mystery of missions. He then walks the sinner in the

ATMOSPHERE of the home (Kingdom) to the DESTINATION of the home (Kingdom). So Christ commands us to say to the lost, *'the Kingdom of God is come nigh unto you.' (Luke 10:9)* And also to pray, *'Thy Kingdom come.' (Matthew 6:10).* Can't you see his footprints all around you? *'Yea, though I walk through the valley of the shadow of death, I will fear no evil: for thou art with me...' (Psalm 23:4)* He shines the brightest where darkness dims the blackest.

THE PARABLE OF THE ABILITY THAT MANIFESTS AROUND SOUL WINNING

It may amaze many that some leave high paying jobs for lower-paying ones. Their reason; they want more challenge. Fulfillment does not only come from what we get to eat but also by what we gather to give. The Church has a four-fold purpose, acronymed WIFE-Worship, Instruction, Fellowship and Evangelism. But of the four the first three belong to the 'inside half' and the last, standing alone, for the 'outside half'. And of the two halves, the most challenging is the only one function belonging to the 'outside half'. It is primarily for this 'outside half' that Christ promised the power for witnessing in Jerusalem, Judea, Samaria and unto the uttermost (farthest) parts of the earth. (Acts 1:8) *'For the promise is unto you, and to your children, and to all that are AFAR OFF, even as many as the LORD our God shall call.' (Acts 2:39).* Why is power promised for witnessing? Because it is the most challenging and I believe it is what Apostle Paul describes as the "work of the ministry" into which every member of Christ's body is called. (Ephesians 4:12). No doubt the father (of the prodigal) had many servants; but until his son returned, the caterers catered for only few, the musicians hanged their instruments and the butcher's knife had not known the throat of a sheep.

How fulfilled they became when the prodigal returned. Soul- winning is the real work of the Church.

A need had arisen in the first church and it had to do with serving tables. So seven strong men were chosen to help serve tables whilst the apostles consecrated to the ministry of the word and prayer. (Acts 6:1-4) These seven were to have Honest Report and to be full of the Holy Ghost and Wisdom. Many of us, men of God, today, do not match these in those outlined qualities. And yet they were only to serve tables. Wait till Philip got to the mission field in Samaria with that same table-serving grace and you will see what a table-serving grace in the church can accomplish on the mission field. (Acts 8:5-8). Our spiritual potentials are primarily meant for soul winning; it is to be directed on the prodigals. Your spiritual strength stretches its full length in Evangelism. Try it. The Church that is not built to push backwards the gates of hell is not Christ's building. (Matthew 16:18) The first church experienced great manifestations of the Holy Spirit in the book of Acts. I have always believed that it was a Church that prayed and also preached the gospel.

THE PROCLAMATION OF THE GOSPEL

INTRODUCTION

There is a story about a research that went on years ago about why children fell off their beds. Of course I have not been able to confirm the source but the story line is still interesting even if it is fiction.

The research was to find an answer to why children fell off their beds in their sleep. The research was fully conducted and the finding was phenomenal. The children who fell off their beds were those who slept at the edge of the bed. In other words those who slept in the middle or at the interior did not have any problem.

Similarly, how we become "Christians" determines where we end. In fact the furthest many can go is the border between the world and Christianity. There are Christians like those who live on the border between two countries; they can easily maneuver to become a citizen of any of the two at any time; especially in our part of the world where proper documentation is almost absent.

I have realized that those Christians that were converted after understanding the cardinal truths of the gospel, had their assurance of salvation intact. Most of these also understood, that there is room for growth in their Christian lives.

I have had an opportunity to ask many "believers" if they are Christians at interviews. The obvious answer has always been a resounding yes. The next question always has been, "How did you become a Christian?" By this time we are closer to the boxing ring. "What makes you sure that you are a Christian?" finally escorts us to the boxing ring. This is not to say everyone who gets the answers correct is a Christian in heart though. But everyone who is genuinely born again must be able to answer these cardinal questions. The more serious aspect is that there are many in the church who erroneously think they are born again. Because such think that one is a Christian by having a Christian name. Others, because they were baptized when they were six weeks. Some, because they do not smoke, drink or chase after women. Many more, because they go to church every Sunday and they have membership cards. And there are those who bought an organ for the church, donated their land for church building or have supported the church and many pastors. As wonderful as all the above are, they are not the means to salvation.

It is only the Gospel that is the POWER of God unto SALVATION. (Romans 1:16) I trust the following will start the self-examination. May the Holy Spirit throw more light.

THE SUPERLATIVES OF THE GOSPEL

There was a certain man in Caesarea called Cornelius...A DEVOUT man... that FEARED GOD with ALL HIS HOUSE, which gave much ALMS to the people, and PRAYED to God ALWAYS. He saw in a VISION... about the ninth hour of the day an ANGEL of God coming in to him, and saying unto him, Cornelius...Thy prayers and thine alms are come up for a MEMORIAL before (IN THE PRESENCE OF) God. And now send men to

Joppa, and call for one Simon, whose surname is Peter: ...he shall tell thee (you) what thou oughtest (ought) to do. (Acts 10:1-6).

Definitions are very important. But many times they are very difficult to arrive at. May the Holy Spirit be our Helper when it comes to biblical definitions and concepts. I have always wondered why one can bestow all his goods to feed the poor and give his body to be burned and STILL not have love. (1 Corinthians 13:3). Yet that is very true. Such are some of the reasons why God looks at our hearts. (1 Samuel 16:7; Matthew 5:28) And if there be any definition we must get right, it must be that of the GOSPEL. Paul says it is the POWER of God unto Salvation. (Romans 1:16) There must be a POWER at work to have anyone SAVED. So John 1:12 says: *'But as many as received Him, to them He gave POWER to become the sons of God, even to them that believe on His name.'*

The Bible gives us the narrative of a very interesting situation: A man sees an angel and the angel directs the man to see another man for direction. In other words, "an angel comes to the earth and points a man towards the earth; and not heaven." The picture is like, "Cornelius, there is something you need to know but the man who can tell you is called Simon Peter; go for him." Hmm. What can a man tell that an angel cannot tell? We have taken the communication of the gospel for granted. God has granted humanity a privilege that is mysterious. *'But though we, or an angel from heaven, preach any other gospel unto you than that which we have preached unto you, let him be accursed.' (Galatians 1:8).*

We have a clear picture here when an angel from God came so close but short of revealing the contents of the gospel.

In our contemporary settings, who needs to hear the Gospel? Definitely a drunkard, a prostitute, an armed robber or a good-for-nothing somebody who needs some motivation to redirect his life. Do you need a visa, is your marriage on rocks, do you need a job, or you are under some spiritual bondage? If Cornelius needed to hear the gospel, what type? Physically he was an European. Visa to any part of the world would not be an issue. Socially, he was a commandant. Financially, he was a philanthropist and spiritually he was very prayerful and God-fearing and had led his whole house along. Above all his devotion had ascended to God's presence as a memorial. What that means...! As a result, an angel was sent to him personally at a time that wasn't a revival meeting. The ordinariness of his devotion was still heaven-attracting. How would you describe such a person? If your devotion culminated in the visitation of an angel, would you need another to talk to you about issues on godliness? Maybe you would immediately start a ministry and set days for consultation. After all you have one angel on your side to unfold mysteries. I have not made any statement yet about how much fees you would be charging for each consultation.

And if Cornelius needed to hear another at all, should it be Peter? Peter had marks of failure engraved all over him. He, on a number of recorded occasions, talks before he thinks. He is known to have openly denied Jesus three times; crowning the third denial with an oath. What did Peter have that was lacking in Cornelius' devotion? Have you met a 'Cornelius' that you concluded did not need to hear the Gospel? If you ever met the girl in Acts 16:16-18, who "prophesied correctly" about

Paul and Silas, wouldn't you fold up your soul-winning skills and seek for spiritual direction yourself? Do we still need the Gospel today? Do current trends in our churches and spiritual gatherings necessitate the clear presentation of the gospel? Read all the revival posters and if you find any speaker titled 'Evangelist' please pray for them; they belong to the "endangered species".

◼ THE SUPERLATIVES OF THE GOSPEL   3A

It was the Jewish Festival of Pentecost. Men from every nation of the then world had gathered in Jerusalem. These representatives were described as devout in religion. (Acts 2:5). Imminently, 3000 souls will be converted out of these devout men. God, on this day poured His Spirit upon 120 disciples. (Acts 2:1-4). But definitely God had the entire world in mind. The phenomenon of the outpouring of God's Spirit can only be described as supernatural. Cloven tongues of fire sat upon each of the 120. Then they were filled with the Holy Spirit and began to speak in tongues. Speaking in an unlearned earthly language is a miracle enough. But the phenomenon was more mysterious than speaking in an unlearned language. ...Every man heard them (the 120) speak at the same time to all of them. And while the 120 were speaking, every language under the sun was heard from the lips of the 120. The scene looked very chaotic. For the audience was confounded (Acts 2:6); they were ALL amazed and marveled (Acts 2:7); they asked, "how?" they asked, "what does this mean? (Acts 2:12); others also mocked and said, "these are drunkards" (Acts 2:13). Then Peter stood up... (Acts 2:14).

The presentation of the gospel is the true climax of every miracle.

Remarkably, at the end of Peter's gospel presentation there was absolute clarity. The response was no more a confusion, a marvel, nor a mockery. Expectantly, their conviction had prompted a need to make a decision. "What shalt we do?" (Acts 2:37). The gospel is the explanation of every supernatural. For Paul describes the gospel as POWER OF GOD. (Romans 1:16, 17). Miracles are not complete without the clear declaration of the gospel. Miracles are special catalysts in inciting a search in the hearts of men. At every miracle the gospel stands up to be heard. The gospel is the tallest miracle.

THE SUPERLATIVES OF THE GOSPEL   3B

On the day of Pentecost, the Holy Spirit fell on the 120 disciples in the form of a mighty rushing wind with tongues of fire resting upon their heads and they spoke in other tongues as the spirit gave them utterance. (Acts 2). Although this was a very supernatural phenomenon, there still arose the need for the clear presentation of the Gospel. And after its detailed presentation, the Israelites asked, "...what shall we do?" Then Peter replied, *'Repent, and be baptized every one of you in the name of Jesus Christ for the REMISSIONS OF SINS, and ye shall receive the gift of the Holy Ghost (Spirit)' (Acts 2:38).* So much had happened that day but the day could not have ended well if Repentance and Remission of sins had not been the climax. *'Then they that gladly received his word were baptized: and the same day there were added unto them about three thousand souls' (Acts 2:41).* They were added and they continued in the Apostles' doctrine and fellowship, and in breaking of bread, and in prayers. (Acts 2:42). The manifestations of the supernatural and the clear presentation of the gospel are inseparable.

'How shall we escape, if we neglect so great salvation; which at first began to be spoken by the LORD, and was confirmed unto us by them that heard him; God also bearing them witness, both with signs and wonders, and with divers miracles, and gifts of the Holy Ghost (Spirit), according to His own will?' (Hebrews 2:3, 4). Amazing partnership: the early Church bore Christ witness and God also bore them witness by confirming their work with "signs, wonders and divers miracles". In Acts 2:22, in Peter's Pentecost Day sermon, he mentioned that Jesus of Nazareth was a man approved of God by "miracles, wonders and signs". So there is no difference in the approval God bestows on Christ and God's confirmation of the Gospel of Christ.

Every notable miracle must be accompanied by a declaration of the Lordship of Christ and His power to remit sins. So Christ says to the man sick of palsy, *'Son, be of good cheer; thy sins be forgiven thee...Arise, take up thy bed and go unto thine (your) house' (Matthew 9:2-6).* That is the reason why the Gospel of John presents the miracles of Christ as signs; they are not an end in themselves; they must be accompanied by a clear presentation of the Gospel.

THE SUPERLATIVES OF THE GOSPEL 4

The scenario begins with Cornelius receiving an angelic visitation from Heaven. Whilst his messengers to fetch Peter were on their way, Peter also falls in a trance as he goes to the housetop to pray. The contents of Peter's vision were introduced by the phrase, "And saw Heaven opened" It was a heavenly experience for both Cornelius and Peter. Exactly by the end of Peter's vision, the men sent by Cornelius were at

"Peter's" gate. Unquestionable manifestation of the supernatural. Peter was so much needed that a holy angel had to be sent from heaven (Acts 10:3,22) to Cornelius in a vision as the Spirit also speaks to Peter in a vision (Acts 10:11-21). Cornelius vision was initiated by an angel; but Peter's, by the Holy Spirit. I believe in the ministration of angels but what happens if a Church (of Christ) relegates the Holy Spirit to the background and it is all about angels?

Peter, with other believers, travel to Caesarea to meet Cornelius as the Spirit had directed. It cannot be denied that the Holy Spirit was part of the team. For He (the Holy Spirit) 'followed' Peter keenly like an athlete waiting for the blast of the gun. He (the Holy Spirit) was readied by Peter's introduction and the highlighting of the essentials of the Gospel:

1. That Christ was the Anointed and ordained of God. (Acts 10:38, 42).

2. That Christ was hanged on the cross and died. (Acts 10:39; 1 Corinthians 15:4).

3. That on the third day, God raised Him up. (Acts 10:40; 1 Corinthians 15:4).

4. That His resurrection was not a secret one; because He appeared unto many. (Acts 10:40, 41; 1 Corinthians 15:5-8).

5. That Christ was the focus of the Old Testament prophets. (Acts 10:43; 1 Corinthians 15:3).

6. Here Peter ends where he ended his sermon on the Day of Pentecost: That through His (Christ's) name whosoever believes in Him shall receive REMISSION OF SINS. (Acts 10:43; 1 Corinthians 15:22).

At this juncture, the "gun blasted" and the Holy Spirit took over. The Gospel had been clearly presented. Christ was received, the Holy Spirit fell and believers were baptized. For about the 100 times that the word "Gospel" appears in the King James Version's New Testament, over 64 mentions are directly accompanied by mostly the word "preached" and on few occasions words like, 'publish', 'testify', 'heard' and few others. The Gospel must be clearly preached.

THE SUPERLATIVES OF THE GOSPEL 5

The Gospel & Sin

The Gospel cannot be preached without the mention of sin. In Acts 3, the Apostle Peter highlights again the essentials of the Gospel. A notable miracle had been performed: A man born paralyzed had been miraculously healed. *'All the people ran together unto them in the porch that is called Solomon's, greatly wondering.'* (Acts 3:11) Here again, Peter clearly presents the Gospel:

1. He presented Christ as the Holy One and the Just. (Acts 3:14).

2. That Christ died. (Acts 3:15).

3. That Christ rose from the dead. (Acts 3:15).

4. That Christ's resurrection was not a secret one; "we are witnesses." (Acts 3:15).

Then once again, he ends where he did in the earlier-mentioned two sermons: *'Repent ye therefore and be converted, that your sins may be blotted out, when the times of refreshing shall come from the presence of the Lord' (3:19).*

The Bible clearly states that *'All have sinned, and come short of the glory of God.' (Romans 3:23)*. This simply means no one can come to God unless his sin is dealt with. And all one can do is to admit his wretchedness in that regard and cry for help. *'O wretched man that I am! Who shall deliver me from this body of death?' (Romans 7:24)*. Yes, Cornelius was a god-fearing man. So why did he need to hear a gospel that concludes with the remission of sins? Because our own righteousness cannot save us. *'But we are all as an unclean thing, and all our righteousness are as filthy as rags...' (Isaiah 64:6)*. All that Heaven is waiting for is the admission of our sins and accepting God's sacrifice for human sin. Cornelius needed God's offer for the remission of sin as we all do. The prodigal son said, "I have sinned" but the elderly one said, *'Lo, these many years do I serve thee (you), neither transgressed I at any time thy (your) commandment...' (Luke 15:29)*. Did you hear him say, "I have never sinned against you". But he is not the only one who was reluctant to admit sin: Adam said, *'The woman whom Thou (you) gavest (gave) to be with me, she gave me of the tree, and I did eat.' And Eve also said, 'The serpent beguiled (deceived) me, and I did eat.' (Genesis 3:12, 13)*. They needed to admit their sin but refused to do so. So when Christ (the last/second Adam) came into this world, he had to SUBSTITUTIONALLY admit sin for Adam's race. *'For He (God) had made Him (Christ) to be sin FOR us who (though he) knew no sin; that we might be made the righteousness of God in Him' (2 Corinthians 5:21)*. So why did Christ need to die? *'For the wages of sin is death; but the gift of God is eternal life through Jesus Christ our Lord.' (Romans 6:23)* It is only in Christ that we die to sin and arise to ETERNAL LIFE. (Romans 6:4).

"For by grace are ye saved through faith; and that not of yourselves: it is the gift of God: Not of works, lest any man should boast' (Ephesians 2:8, 9).

"For God so loved the world, that He gave His only begotten Son, that whosoever believeth (believes) in Him (Christ) should not perish, but have everlasting life." (John 3:16). Amen.

THE SUPERLATIVES OF THE GOSPEL FINALS

"And the angel of the Lord spake (spoke) unto Philip, saying, Arise, and go toward the south unto the way that goeth (goes) down from Jerusalem to Gaza, which is desert. And he arose and went: and, behold, a man of Ethiopia, an eunuch of great authority under Candace queen of the Ethiopians, who had the charge of all her treasure, and had come for to worship.' (Acts 8:26, 27).

Once again we see an angel instructing a human to perform a task you would have expected the angel to do himself. Why are the angels standing behind the scenes as coaches and cheering humans to do evangelism? And isn't it amazing that angels start the evangelism arrangement but as it gets closer to the gospel, it is the Holy Spirit that plays the pivotal role? (Acts 8:29; 10:44).

These angels have not been saved before and salvation for the human soul was solely accomplished by the Godhead. The saved can testify better about salvation. Humans occupy a position in God's economy that remains mysterious to the angelic realm. You had thought they hold the key to all spiritual mysteries. Yes, the gospel occupies a higher realm than that of the angels because it is the gospel of Christ, the Son of God. But at times we present the gospel in such a way that other humans, not even angels, become higher than the gospel. That is when we re-design the gospel as a visa-acquiring, a husband-finding, a miracle-claiming code. We are causing many to fall out of the bracket of those who need the gospel. Does the gospel have a home in the heart of a wealthy, healthy, and yet with a filthy soul? For a man's soul (without Christ) is as filthy as a rag. (Isaiah 64:6) Here was a healthy man as far as the distance he has traveled is concerned. He definitely does not look like somebody to whom the attainment of a visa would be classified as a miracle. As for money, he was probably the highest paid official in Ethiopia at the time. Religiously he had traveled all this distance to Israel to come and worship. Having achieved all the above, he did not understand what Isaiah was saying about Christ.

"How can I (understand), except some man should guide me?' (Acts 8:31) You see, the gospel of Christ is weightier than wealth, higher than health and soul-saving than Israel.

"...He was led as a sheep to the slaughter; and like a lamb dumb before his shearer, so He opened not his mouth: In his humiliation his judgment was taken away: and who shall declare His generation? For His life is taken from the earth. And the eunuch answered Philip and said... "of whom speaketh (speaks) the prophet this?" ...Then Philip opened his mouth, and began at the same scripture, and preached unto him Jesus. And as they went on their way (further on), they came (arrived) unto a certain water: and the eunuch said, see, here is water; what doth (does) hinder me to be baptized? And Philip said, If thou (you) believeth (believe) with all thine (your) heart, thou mayest (may). And he (the eunuch) answered and said, I BELIEVE THAT JESUS CHRIST IS THE SON OF GOD ...and they went both into the water...; and he (Philip) baptized him (the eunuch). And when they were come up out of the

water, the Spirit of the Lord caught away Philip...and he (the eunuch) went on his way rejoicing.' (Acts 8:32-39).

Let us carry to the world the Good News that bring great joy. (Luke 2:10).

THE
PROPHETIC IN TODAY'S CHURCH

INTRODUCTION

The series on the prophetic themselves contains their own introductions. Just a little explanation on the term 'prophet'. J. Sidlow Baxter in his book, EXPLORE THE BOOK, writes the following: "...prophecy is not merely prediction. The common idea today is that prophecy is wholly a matter of foretelling the future, but that idea is erroneous. It is founded on the wrong etymology; for the 'pro' in "prophet" is not that which means 'beforehand' as in the word 'provide', but that which means 'in place of' as in the word 'pronoun' The remainder of the word 'prophet' is from the Greek 'phemi', which means to speak. So a prophet is the one who speaks in place of another. Thus, when Moses quailed at the thought of being sent to Israel in Egypt, on account of his supposed inability as a speaker, God said to him: *'See, I have made thee a god unto Pharaoh; and Aaron thy brother shall be thy prophet.' (Exodus 7:1)* Aaron was to be his brother's prophet in that he was to speak in his name, and in place of him." (Page 207)

Baxter, on the same page, further explains that "whilst all prediction is prophecy, not all prophecy is prediction.

The work of the prophet therefore, whether by fore-telling (prediction) or forth-telling (declaration of truth) is to point to God. In Elijah's day, the people proclaimed that, *'The LORD, He is God.' (1 Kings 18:39).* Moses cautioned Israel that, *'...man does not live by bread alone, but man lives by everything that proceeds out of the mouth of God.' (Deuteronomy 8:3; Matthew 4:4).* Isaiah said, *'Woe is me...for I am a man of unclean lips; for mine eyes have seen the king, the LORD of hosts.' (Isaiah 6:5)* John the

Baptist said, *'He must increase but I must decrease.' (John 3:30)* The prophetic ministry, primarily, is to draw man's attention to God. Anything short of that is not prophetic: *"If a prophet, or one who foretells by dreams, appears among you and announces to you a miraculous sign or wonder, and if the sign or wonder of which he has spoken TAKES PLACE (is fulfilled), and (but) he says, 'Let us follow other gods' (gods you have not known) 'and let us worship them,' you must not listen to the words of the prophet or dreamer (seer). The LORD your God is testing you to find out whether you love Him with all your heart and with all your soul. It is the LORD your God you must follow, and Him you must revere. Keep His commands and obey Him; serve Him and hold fast to Him. That prophet or dreamer must be put to death because he has preached rebellion against the LORD your God, who brought you out of Egypt and redeemed you from the land of slavery; he has tried to turn you from the way the LORD your God commanded you to follow. You must purge the evil from among you.' (Deuteronomy 13:1-5)*

Of course we are not to kill false prophets today because we are not under a theocracy today, but still turning people's heart away from God is a serious sin. So the yardstick is not whether a prophet's predictions come to pass or not; it is whether he draws people closer to God in reverence or he turns their hearts away from God. Judge for yourself

Gift of Prophecy [1]

One day, I was at the mechanic's shop and they were discussing the latest prophecies in town. These included Ex-President Robert Mugabe dying in the year 2018. A prophecy even a drunkard can declare. The man is graciously old; hence the high probability. The other man in the conversation said this prophet once prophesied that no "Atta" (twin) can ever be a president but the late President John Evans Atta Mills won. This young man added that as soon as Atta Mills won the presidency, he left the Prophet's church. One reason for all these is that we have left the major criteria of I Timothy 3 & Titus 3 as the standard for ministry and we are now replacing them with fulfillment of predictions. The Old Testament concept of testing a Prophet by the fulfillment of his word is set within a very broad concept. So it is dangerous to single out the fulfillment of prophecies as the ultimate yardstick of trustworthiness in ministry.

Today many pastors are in a rush to prophesy to seek authentication and recognition. Someone rightly said on the radio that because of this need for recognition, if the Prophet or the Pastor says you will die, he will do everything to make sure you die. So that he will be a known prophet. But that is not the only reason. Many people go to Church and until the Prophet calls him or her forward to reveal some unknown details about them, there was 'no church'.

I guess the offering also becomes substantial to the extent of the prophetic ministration. "Go deep, Papa" is an encouraging response from some recipients of prophetic revelations in South- Eastern Africa. It is therefore obvious in view of the above and others, that many men of God are under constant pressure to prophesy. Besides, a successful prophetic ministry 'feels' good.

My only concern is that the prophetic gift is so important that it should not be abused to the extent that people begin to make mockery of it and eventually reject their appropriateness in the salvation of souls. The prophetic belongs to the miraculous and miracles are a revelation of the Holy and the Righteous God. People ought to go beyond the prophetic and see God. That is why the Gospel according to John referred to miracles as signs. They pointed to the Savior. (John 20:30).

Gift of Prophecy [2]

One of the reasons for the chaos that has ruined the beautiful prophetic field is that we have not been able to define who a prophet is and what prophecy is.

Many spiritually-looking exercises have been labeled as prophecy when they are not. And some notable prophets by virtue of their unfaithfulness to God have crossed into divination. And of course, there are false prophets.

The challenge is that the average believer has struggled with identifying a true prophetic ministration. We will need to crawl in these series to effectively do justice to this topic; otherwise, we will cut down both the wheat and the tares.

Today, let me narrate to you some real life "prophetic" scenarios: I was at a church when a prophet prophesied. He told me, William Okyere, that a friend will send me a BMW from the USA in three months. This was around 2005/6. He also prophesied that a woman had been healed of fibroid. He challenged that if the woman goes to the hospital and the fibroid was still there, he will "put his Bible down."

Interestingly I was the Dean of Manna Bible Institute when the woman came to surgically remove the fibroid at the Manna Mission Hospital.

I am still waiting for my BMW.

Gift of Prophecy [3]

This is not to say there are no genuine prophecies. There are, and many can testify to that. In fact, the reason for this series is to help guide us to respond appropriately to the prophetic ministry. I gave examples in Gift of prophecy 2 just to alert us that the prophetic field needs to be entered into with a lot of discernment and spiritual caution.

Now, how does God relate to prophecy? The Bible - God's major way of speaking to man- is about 75% prophecy. In other words, God is a Prophet. So is His Son, our Lord, and Savior Jesus Christ. God is therefore very interested in the prophetic. Before we outline God's attitude to prophecy, let us outline few 'elements' of prophecy that in themselves may not always be prophetic.

1. PREDICTION- Many predictions can come true. If I say that a pregnant woman will give birth to a baby girl, it is in fact 50% probable. This could be prophecy but it could also be a mere prediction.

2. So are abilities to have insight into a situation, inspirational utterances, even in biblical wordings.

A clear example is in *Acts 16:16-18 "And it came to pass, as we went to prayer, a certain damsel possessed with a spirit of divination met us…The same followed Paul and us and cried saying, these men are the servants of the Most High God, which shew unto us the way of salvation. And this she did MANY DAYS. But Paul, being grieved, turned and said to the spirit, I command thee in the name of Jesus Christ to come out of her. And he came out that same hour."*

Why did this have to continue for many days? It had every appearing element of prophecy. Besides, it was a prayer environment. This may have passed for a prophecy until Paul got grieved from within. This is to establish the fact that it is not every "prophetic utterance" that will pass the test of prophecy.

Gift of Prophecy [4]

We have mentioned that God is a Prophet. Well, the Major Prophet and Prophet 1 positions are already occupied by men. I do not know the prophetic positions available to God now. Because God is a Prophet, the Bible, the written word of God, is in itself prophetic. So why do we need the prophetic ministry? In the first place, the prophetic ministry does not replace the written word of God. What does it do then? It CONFIRMS the word. In other words, there must be God's word settled in us for us to respond either positively or negatively to any "prophetic utterance".

Secondly, it CUSTOMIZES the word. In other words, God's intention for you in His word is made very personal just as it happens in our personal devotions. You see, it is so encouraging when God's word becomes personal.

Thirdly, the prophetic CLARIFIES the word. Prophecy has the ability to break down God's word to make it relevant for today's living. That was the focus of many of the Old Testament prophets. They said things like, *"True fasting is to give your food to the poor". (Isaiah 58).*

Finally the prophetic can directly COMMUNICATE God's word. I have heard many prophetic sermons. In fact, preaching itself can be classified as prophesying. That is why you go to church and after hearing the sermon, you suspect your spouse or friend has leaked your personal details to the pastor.

The Bible student can realize a lot of preaching elements in the works of the Old Testament prophets. I believe all these is what Paul says in *1 Corinthians 14:3: "He that prophesieth (prophesies) SPEAKETH UNTO MEN (communication), TO EDIFICATION (customize) and EXHORTATION (clarification) and COMFORT (confirmation)."*

Your question as well as mine is: Why is Christianity not getting better with the proliferation of the "prophetic" ministry? It is because many prophetic ministries are not building on the word of God; they are rather replacing it. Some of the things you hear are horrible. One time I requested from God that if He has changed His Word He should let us know. Because at times, it is so confusing. Previously, the prophetic ministry was scanty but Christianity was more solid. Because in those days, the word of God was not replaced, the ministry was built upon it. God's word is a solid foundation for ministry.

"Therefore whosoever heareth (hears) these sayings of mine, and doeth them, I will liken him unto a wise man, which built his house upon a rock. (Mathew 7:24).

Gift of Prophecy [5]

I have always had a position on people seeking prophetic ministration: "People have issues." Many times I hear pastors lambast their congregation for roaming from one prophet to another prophet. Why won't they, if every night a spirit comes to sleep with a woman and as a result she cannot enjoy sex with the husband and children are not being born; or none of the children in a family are able to go pass junior high; another literally hears voices every time; another's sickness is out of orthodox medicine's reach; and unexplainable encroachment of poverty.

Do you expect all these people to remain calmly seated in a church where the pastor does not even know them? The woman with the issue of blood did the same thing. She moved as long and as far as her money could afford. (Luke 8:43, 44) Her resilience finally brought her to Jesus and she was made whole. We should not hide behind statements like, "my ministry is a teaching ministry".

The greatest teacher was also a miracle worker. Besides, many of the miracles and prophetic ministration are congregationally hatched. Have you asked yourself why notable miracles happen at big crusades? Do you think it was only the man upstage? God is always touched by the plight of the needy multitude (Mark 6:34) and also there is power in congregational prayers. Our Lord's model prayer is corporately structured. All I am saying is that every church must be "prophetically" caring. Jesus, many times, narrowed his attention to individuals who were wretched, poor, non-entities and ministered to them. Let us attach the same attitude to people's needs. The announcements are getting too long. Some of us may not know how it feels for a prophet to call an individual out of the multitudes and begin to address the person's problems. *"Come, see a man, which told me all things that I ever did: Is not this the Christ?" (John 4:29)* When people have been ministered to, they will minister to others.

Gift of Prophecy [6]

The Bible is God's primary means of speaking to man. So it is not out of place to say that "God has already spoken what He speaks today." Many Christians are pursuing the prophetic as though there is something left unsaid. In our Era, the prophetic is supposed to be a congregational experience. *"How is it then, brethren? When ye come together, EVERY ONE OF YOU hath a psalm, hath a doctrine, hath a tongue, hath a revelation, hath an interpretation."*

"Let all things be done unto edifying." (1Corinthians 14:26). What this means is that the congregation is a "market" for the batter 'trade' of spiritual gifts. Everybody has a spiritual gift or more to offer. Hundreds of thousands of people all gathering to receive from one person or appearing to do so make the church malfunction. Yes, the leader will stand out but the congregation should not bow out. In other words, congregational giftings should be encouraged and recognized as supportive ministries. Coming back to the fact that God has already spoken all there is about you: Jesus summarizes the two major intentions towards every human soul in John 10:10: *"The thief cometh not, but for (except) to steal, and to kill, and to destroy; I have come that they*

might (you will) have life, and that they might (you will) have it more abundantly."

Everything about any person that will ever be revealed falls under one of these two headings: Christ's intention and that of Satan's. A dear sister did come to me with the concern about some revelation about death. I did not rubbish it as untrue, but I also clarified that it is not new. Looking at your life you will realize that you have always been on Satan's death list.

I personally got attacked by armed robbers on a highway. I almost lost one of my eyes. I have blacked out a number of times. I was sick most of my childhood. So if anybody tells me I am going to die this year, I will tell him, in fact, I should have died many years ago. In fact, I needed such a prophet to have told me this in March 2005. If another tells me God is going to bless me, it confirms what is all over in the Bible. (Psalm 1) And if there is any prophetic direction, none surpasses *1Peter 5:8 "Be sober, be vigilant; because your adversary the devil, as a roaring lion, walketh about, seeking whom he may devour."*

If it is your auntie who is 'doing' you, it is the same thing as Peter is saying. In other words, that your auntie may be the devil's claw or teeth. So it is important that we see the Bible as our primary prophetic material.

We are all on the devil's permanent death list; let us daily caution our lives prayerfully: *"See then that ye walk circumspectly, not as fools, but as wise, redeeming the time, because the days are evil. Wherefore be ye not unwise, but understanding what the will of the Lord is." (Ephesians 5:15-17)*

And if one prophesies blessing, all we need to do is to daily walk on the paths of His righteousness where goodness and mercy will follow us daily. (Psalm 23).

Let me make it clear that I believe in the prophetic. In other words, I do not believe that the gifts of the Spirit ceased with the completion of the Bible.

Let me here define PROPHECY:

The Hebrew root word for prophecy is 'nabi' which literary means- to bubble forth. Jesus gave a picture of this in John 7:38; He that believeth on me, as the scripture hath said, OUT OF HIS BELLY SHALL FLOW RIVERS OF LIVING WATER. The next verse explains that this statement Jesus made had everything to do with the Holy Spirit.

From this root word, we get the name 'Barnabas'. 'Bar' always means 'son' and the second part of the name is rooted in 'nabi'; that is why Barnabas means "son of consolation" It means that Barnabas always bubbled forth consolation. Prophecy always has consolation at the center. Even if it predicts doom, it must always end with the assurance that "God is in control".

The book of Isaiah has always been described as the miniature Bible. It has 66 chapters as the Bible has 66 books. Its first 39 chapters appears like the Bible's Old Testament of 39 books and its last 27 appears like the Bible's 27 books of the New Testament.

The first 39 chapters predict devastation but the second 27 predicts consolation. Beautifully the second 27 which begins in chapter 40 starts with: *"Comfort ye, comfort ye My people."* So every prophecy, no matter the wording, must exhibit God's love and His divine interest in our welfare. This goes with the popular saying, *"He reveals to redeem."* So prophesying is not to score prophetical points, but rather to link the recipient to God's love.

When Alice got imprisoned in Senegal, I had a prophetic ministration and it started with: *"God says I should tell you He loves you."* At this time, I had mental battles - God what have I done wrong? I was expecting a doomsday prophecy but God settled me. Why do you think God follows us through the fire and the waters? (Isaiah 43:2).

He shares our pain. If God ever reveals you are going to die and should you die, His wish for you is to die in His arms. For God so loved the world... (John 3:16) The Corinthian church was God's problem church and yet one of the greatest literary formulations of the merciful nature of God was penned to them: *Blessed be God, even the FATHER of our Lord Jesus Christ, the Father of MERCIES, and the God of ALL COMFORT. Who comforteth us in ALL our tribulation... (2Corinthians 1:3, 4)*

I prophesy to you today that you will be comforted; SPIRITUALLY, MENTALLY, EMOTIONALLY and PHYSICALLY. God is not against you; He is for you. Bless you.

Gift of Prophecy [7]

I tried to define prophecy in our previous write-up. We concluded with the fact that the purpose of New Testament prophecy is to comfort the people of God.

Let us move to a more technical definition of the gift of prophecy: It is a spontaneous declaration of a revelation (in a seed form) dropped in a believer's heart for God's people. The reason I inserted the term 'seed' is that the process involved in the gift of prophecy is paraphrasing in nature. What it means is that two people can receive the same revelation but the more mature believer will bring out a higher spiritual content.

Just like preaching, two people may use the same scripture and yet the exhortation level may not be the same. And also the vessel may not always have the entire revelation; He or she is prompted by the initial 'deposit' and the rest flows as the vessel yields.

Getting the definition right is what cessationists (those who believe the spiritual gifts ceased with the completion of scripture) get it wrong: The gift of prophecy, like the one practiced in the Church of Corinth, was not meant to be a part of the process of completing the Bible, it was part of the spiritual dynamics of maturing the members of Christ's body. (1Corinthians 14:4). He that prophesieth edifies the Church. It never said he that prophesieth completes the scriptures.

The work of completing the Bible was assigned by the Holy Spirit to the Apostles; not the New Testament prophets. And saying the gifts were needed at the time when the scripture was not complete does not resonate with scripture. The early Church saw the Old Testament scriptures as complete. For the New was in the Old concealed. The Bible student will easily realize that the end of the book of Revelation resembles the beginning of the book of Genesis in detail.

So the work of the Canon of Scripture was given to the Old Testament Prophets and the New Testament Apostles by an act of God that will never be repeated. It is called INSPIRATION.   That is why the early church continued in the Apostle's doctrine. That is why a prophetic declaration, like that in the Corinthian Church, was to be judged or weighed. (1Corinthians 14:29). But when it comes to the inspired New Testament, it was locked when the book of Revelation was completed; nobody can add and nobody can subtract. (Revelation 22:18, 19) And nobody dares bring the inspired word to a level of being judged. (2Timothy 3:16).

We can, therefore, conclude the following:

1. Congregational prophesying was not practiced to complete the scriptures.

2. The prophetic grows and perfects by maturity.

3. Immaturity has the ability to short-circuit the impact of the prophetic.

4. The 'prophet' needs mature others to biblically weigh his prophetic contents.

So any believer who receives revelation or prophesies should not equate himself to Peter, Paul and other NT writers and anyone who receives prophecy must prayerfully weigh it.

Gift of Prophecy [8]

The Prophetic Attitude:

We have mentioned a couple of times that God is a Prophet just as He is a Pastor (shepherd). I sincerely believe that if the prophetic is going to benefit us we must carefully observe the source of the prophetic and the One who ordains all prophets. God must have an exemplary way of handling the prophetic that is worth emulating.

The Language of Intimacy

God has no competitor and therefore fearless. He is above all. He is not a man-pleaser. His word is final. Jesus confronted the Pharisees fearlessly but on several occasions taught in parables. On a number of occasions, He only explained when He was with the disciples and when they themselves had asked for the meaning. Truth, like gold, is mined. Truth, like medicine, is taken in dosages. The Psalmist (Psalm 91) calls where God dwells a 'secret place'. Jesus confirms this by emphasizing 'closet' prayer. (Matthew 6:6).

At another time the God of lightning and thunder decided to speak to the prophet of fire in a still small voice. (1Kings 19:12, 13). I believe the most powerful way that God speaks to us is when we are alone with Him. In other words, His highest medium is to speak to us directly. Of course, there is a place for public prophetic discourses but the most effective, the most permanent and the most profound is when God speaks to us personally. The tabernacle symbolizes Christ who is our place in God. The structure of the tabernacle indicates that there are inner chambers in Christ.

Let us come to your house. The farthest some can reach is at the gate. Another will be privileged to step into your compound. Trusted relations can make it to your living room and a selected few can see your bedroom. God, until Christ, lived in the Tabernacle. The Levites (a tribe) ended at the compound; the priests (a family) managed to the Holy place; the High Priest (a person) made it to the Holy of Holies.

So you see the holiest place in God is attained through intimacy. Do you realize that the numbers were reduced as man drew closer to God's Holy of Holies? A tribe reduced to a family and a family, a person? Hmm, many are called... What is God teaching us? Few are those ready to pay the price that leads to intimacy with God. The sharpest prophetic details come to those who tarry at the secret place. The good news: Jesus' death tore the veil that isolated the Holy of Holies from top to bottom. (Matthew 27:51). The Holy of Holies is opened! You can get there...

Gift of Prophecy [9]

The Language of Symbolism

We have discussed the language of Intimacy. One other means that God communicates with us when it comes to revelations and the prophetic is in the language of symbols. Symbols feature prominently in God's prophetic dealings with His people. All of Joseph's dreams that was linked to his world were in symbols.

First, it was sheaves (Genesis 37:7). Secondly, it was the sun, the moon and eleven stars (37:9). In interpreting the dreams of Joseph's fellow prisoners; the first's revelation was represented by a vine and its three branches which represented three days. Interestingly the second's three days were represented by three white baskets and his death was represented by birds eating 'pastries' from baskets on his head. (Genesis 40) Also in Pharaoh's dream famine was represented by lean kine (cattle) swallowing up fat ones and seven withered ears of maize eating up seven fat ones. In this dream, seven fat kine (cattle) and seven good ears of maize all represented seven fruitful years.

This concept repeats in the books of Daniel, Ezekiel, Revelation and many other prophetic narrations in the Bible. In the Book of Revelation, Jesus was presented both as a lamb and a lion (Revelation 5:1-10). These phenomena calls for a lot of caution in revelation and prophetic interpretations. One time, in a dream, I saw one particular Christian leader inviting me to come and work in his Church but that later ended up being another leader of the same caliber. So the leader I saw represented the classification of the person who was to invite me. This must tell you that your mother chasing you in a dream (if at all) may be a warning that somebody as loving as your mother may want to harm you. It may not necessarily mean your mother in person.

Symbolism in the Book of Revelation also teaches us that the fearless God is not as blunt as other prophets today. He decorates prophetic truth in symbols. Looking at Joseph alone, one can realize that different symbols can mean the same thing at a given time, yet the same thing can mean different things at another time. Interpretations of revelations should not be rushed. Be careful of anyone who attempts to interpret revelations impulsively.

It may end up in disaster. Having the revelation is one thing and interpreting correctly is distinctly another.

To interpret Nebuchadnezzar's dream, Daniel asked for time to seek God's face and he did not do it alone. (Daniel 2:16, 17). Let the prophets speak two or three, and let the other judge. (1 Corinthians 14:29) It means no one prophet is immune from error. And let not that error land on your head or in your marriage. Seek personal confirmations from God in intimate prayer.

Gift of Prophecy [10]

Prophetic Language in Fragments

"What is the outcome then, brethren? When you assemble, each one has a psalm, has a teaching, has a revelation, has a tongue, has an interpretation. Let all things be done for edification." (I Corinthians 14:26).

Now in Ghana, the prophetic is the thing. But until we understand how the word of God is packaged, we will be spiritually malnourished. For when believers meet, God speaks to members of His body through many others. In Isaiah 28:13, God was speaking to the Israelites precept upon precept: line upon line; a little here and a little there. I believe no one preaching or prophetic revelation is totally complete in itself. The next is intended to explain the previous. All ministrations that come to us add up to God's thought for us. (Jeremiah 29:11) It is, therefore, a disaster to narrow God's will for our lives only from the prophetic point of view.

Will it be out of place to rephrase I Corinthians 14:26 as:

A little psalm, a little teaching, precept upon precept; a revelation here, a tongue there; an interpretation line upon line; will my people be edified. To live only on the prophetic is one of the highest forms of spiritual malnourishment.

In our next series, we will understand that the proper nourishment of the Church is given to the Pastor and Teacher. On some occasions, I have observed a church service and I see spiritual manifestations but I do not see an all-round church. On such occasions, congregation worship is obviously absent. If you are not among the fortunate ones to be directly told that God will multiply your business, you may go home with no word in your heart.

Joseph had a prophetic revelation that one day his brothers will bow before him. That was, however, a small portion of God's total plan. "How to overcome temptation"; Integrity, "faithfulness", "caring for others when all of you are suffering" were needed to propel Joseph into God's prophetic intention. It may not be surprising that these virtues were nurtured at "Sunday School" or even parental advice. And yet they were as important as prophetic declarations. You realize that these "non-prophetic" parts of God's total plan were a solid foundation for the fulfillment of the prophecy.

For the effective work of the ministry by Christians, for the highest form of unity, for growth into the full stature, for stability in doctrine, all hands (apostolic, prophetic, evangelistic, pastoral and teaching) must be on deck. Many Christians today are only selecting the prophetic. The prophetic has its place but does not occupy all places. A little prophetic here and a little teaching there...precept upon precept; line upon line.

Who is a Prophet? [1]

A quick glance at some Old Testament prophets:

Prophet Moses was a lawgiver; Prophet Samuel was a nation-building and king-making prophet; Elijah called a backslidden nation back to God; Isaiah was a revelatory teaching prophet. So the Old Testament prophets ministered from a variety of angles. Of course, there were miraculous manifestations to confirm their calls. But when it comes to the New Testament Church, we have simply identified our prophets simply with the gift of prophecy. But it is worth stating that prophesying does not make one a prophet. In fact, some so-called prophets are simply operating in the word of knowledge and the word of wisdom.

The other leadership ministries like apostles, evangelists, pastors, and teachers also have had their definitions locked up in traditional renderings. Some of these definitions are as cheap as explaining a pastor as soft-spoken and an evangelist as a hyper. Practically, it can be the other way round. But before we discuss further, I wish to lay down few Bible-understanding principles:

1. The Bible is its best interpreter. In other words, if you find any difficult information in the Bible, it is basically in the same Bible that you will find an opener.

2. Every book of the Bible is its best interpreter. So if you come across a difficult biblical concept, the first place to seek enlightenment must be in the book itself. For example, one will not understand the seriousness of Nebuchadnezzar's image until one is aware that Daniel had explained an image he (Nebuchadnezzar) saw in his dream. Babylon was represented by the image's head. That made Nebuchadnezzar's kingdom transient. But he wanted his kingdom to be forever like God. So he built a physical image that was all gold as against the one he saw in his dream that had only the head as gold. If everyone had bowed to that image, it will be equal to worshipping him as God. He needed to be defied. And that is what the Hebrew boys did. You must now understand why the Son of God joined them in the fire. They had glorified the God of Heaven.

3. If you want to understand any word in a Bible chapter, the meaning is not far away. It is either hidden in that chapter, or the previous or the following. Especially when you see starters like; now, so, hence, wherefore, therefore, but, since. The epistle of Hebrews is a key example. You will not appreciate chapter 11 unless you have read chapter 10. Neither will you appreciate chapter 12 unless you read chapter 11.

All the above can be summarized as understanding the Bible within its context. I believe the average Christian is aware that the Bible in its original form did not have chapters and verses. It was very flowing in content. Some of the books of the Bible were written as letters. So many times a continuous or unbreakable reading makes more meaning.

Who is a Prophet? [2]

But unto every one of us is given grace according to the gift of Christ. Wherefore he saith," When he ascended up on high, he led captivity captive and gave gifts unto MEN...And he gave some, apostles; and some, prophets; and some, evangelists; and some, pastors and teachers; For the perfecting of the saints, for the work of the ministry, for the edifying of the body of Christ: *Till we all come to the unity of the faith, and of the knowledge of the Son of God, unto a perfect man, unto the measure of the stature of the fullness of Christ: Till we henceforth be no more children, tossed to and fro, and carried about with every wind of doctrine, by the sleight of men, and cunning craftiness, whereby they lie in wait to deceive;" (Ephesians 4:7, 8, 11-13).*

The ministry gifts as outlined above are those that are called the five-fold ministries. Reading carefully, these gifts are a means to an end. They are not an end in themselves. Their effectiveness can be measured by the overall growth of the body of Christ.

Areas to look at:

1. Perfecting of Saints.

2. Work of ministry

4. Edifying of the Body of Christ.

5. Unity of Faith

6. Revelation of Christ

7. Growing into His stature

8. Stability in doctrine and teaching

The list continues.

Who is a Prophet? [3]

In our previous discussions, we laid some foundations. We have also looked at the main passage in Ephesians chapter 4 that outlined the ministry gifts namely Apostles, Prophets, Evangelists, Pastors, and Teachers. The following foundation is also very important. VERBAL INSPIRATION means that every word in the original scriptures is inspired. In other words, it is not only the ideas that are inspired but also the words that formulate the ideas are also inspired. Inspiration means God's breath is in His word. Jesus said the words that I speak to you, they are spirit and life. (John 6:63).

That is why the Bible is able to impart life. What this means is that translations are important. Translators ought to stay faithful to the original words. All the translated versions have their strengths. But let me highlight one of the strengths of the King James Version. They stayed so faithful to the original words to the extent that if they ever added a word in the translation to clarify the meaning of a sentence they put those added words in italics to let the reader know that such words were not in the original and that it was inserted for clarification. So at times, do the exercise of reading some passages without the italics. That is if you are a King James user.

Secondly, pay particular attention to biblical words. So let us pay particular attention to some passages in Ephesians chapter 4. Verse 8 reads: *...When he ascended up on high, He led captivity captive and He gave gifts unto MEN.*

Note: Not the CHURCH. In other words, these gifts were meant for the whole of the human population; not only the Church. It is just like John 3:16 says *"For God so loved the WORLD– the whole human population– that He gave us the gift of His only begotten Son."* So God gave Christ to the world and Christ also, in turn, gave the Apostles, the Prophets, the Evangelists, Pastors and Teachers to the whole human population. So those of us who find ourselves in these ministries are a GIFT to the world. That is why we DO NOT CHARGE money for our ministries; we are so important.

Who Is A Prophet? [4]

We ended on the note that the ministrations of the ministry gifts are not to have price tags. But God also warns us against leaving such ministry gifts hungry. (1 Corinthians 9:9, 11; 1Timothy 5:17, 18).

We have established that the ministry gifts were given to MEN; not only to the Church. Ephesians 4:11 reads: *And He gave some (of men)*

Apostles; and some (of men) Prophets; and some (of men) Evangelists; and some (of men) Pastors and Teachers. Having the definition of Verbal Inspiration in mind, the keen observer will easily recognize that the word "SOME" appears four times in this passage.

The literal rendering indicates that Christ divided the human population into four and to each of the four He gave a gift. So we are now seeking a clue from the same book of Ephesians if we will see any four-fold structure: *"For we wrestle not against FLESH and BLOOD (human population) but against Principalities, against Powers, against the Rulers of the Darkness of this World, against Spiritual Wickedness in High Places. (Ephesians 6:12).*

1. Satan has a four-fold demonic strategy. It means Satan has also divided the world into four. So Our Lord Jesus, as outlined in Ephesians 4:11, is sending us to meet Satan boot-for-boot.

2. It means that in Jesus' case He gave one group two ministry gifts-Pastors and Teachers.

3. From Ephesians 6:12, and linking up with Ephesians 4:11, it means these ministry gifts are to lead in warfare; they are not a way of acquiring wealth.

4. So where Principalities attack, Christ sends the Apostle; where Powers attack, Christ sends, the Prophet; where the Rulers of the Darkness of this World attack, Christ sends the Evangelist; and where Spiritual Wickedness in High Places attack, Christ sent Pastors and Teachers.

5. We Apostles, Prophets, Evangelists, Pastors and Teachers have been called unto people. When all of us decide to go prophetic, we would leave eighty percent of the ministry gifts non-functional.

Who is a prophet? [5]

We are trying to stay in Ephesians and do all our definitions here. Definitions of the ministry gifts are highlighted in many parts of the New Testament but we want to squeeze into only Ephesians.

So, if the Apostle is sent to confront the Principality, then what is the Apostle's function? And what is a Principality? A Prince or Principal simply means 'first'. So a principality over a community simply says I came here first, and none other is coming here. He holds the community in poverty, sickness, immorality, curses, idolatry etc. Anything that will bring deliverance from such strongholds, especially the Church, the principality will fight tooth and nail. You must hereby understand why Churches find it difficult to thrive in some communities.

Well, do not forget that in Christ's spiritual economy, the apostle is also a kind of a first. (1Corinthians 12:28) So the one representing the true Alpha faces the one representing the fake first. Please don't rush to be an apostle now. We are talking about fallow-breaking warfare here. Not spiritually light ribs. Why do you think Paul says he fought beasts in Ephesus? (1Corinthians 15:32) Any place that is a stronghold, we must find a notable apostolic gift to lead us in breaking the fallow ground.

Whilst a Principality says, "this is where I belong", a Power, as in Ephesians 6:12, simply says "this is where you belong." Powers infiltrate through deceptive cultural practices. People serve Satan unawares. So the Principality watches over the LOCALITY and the Power influences the people's MENTALITY. An 'unconverted' kingdom is held by Principalities and Powers. That is why when Satan was "offering" Jesus the Kingdoms of the World, he had to take Him to a dimension where Jesus could recognize the physical locations of the kingdoms of the world and then demand worship which would have captivated His mind in bondage. (Matthew 4:4).

For whatsoever we worship captivates our mind. The Prophet's confrontation with Powers is also to make sure that although we are in this world we would not be OF this world. That is, to shield Christians from worldliness. So whilst principalities resist light from coming to the people, powers keep the people from seeking the light. That is why people can travel thousands of miles from their localities and yet their cultural origins are hardly out of them. Their minds are 'power' fully captivated. Going by Ephesians, the New Testament prophetic gift is far higher than operating in the word of wisdom and the word of knowledge. That is why many of the Old Testament prophets were called unto Kings and nations and they spoke against the evils of their day especially IDOLATRY.

The Old Testament prophets operated in high-level wisdom. And of course, they also prophesied; fore-telling and forth telling. Some were lawgivers, some established nations and some were deep-rooted teachers of God's word especially where there is doctrinal contention.

Elijah delivered a whole nation from Baal worship and Israel finally proclaimed, "The Lord He is God". The mental hold was broken.

.

Who is a Prophet? [6]

The same principles applied in discussing the term "Prophet' will be used in discussing the other ministry gifts.

The third ministry gift is an Evangelist. His opposing counterpart from the demonic world is called Rulers of the Darkness of this World. Simply put, they keep the world in darkness. They "supply" darkness whilst the Evangelist "supplies" light. The Evangelist is God's gift to the dark world. Jesus did not leave the unbelieving world without a gift. That is why these gifts were not given only to the Church but to MEN which includes the Church. After all, the Church's source of population is the unbelieving world. How then can God love the Church without loving the world?

Then to the last grouping, specifically the Church (especially in the local setting) our Lord gives the Pastor and the Teacher. Should you be surprised why, many times, these two gifts reside in a single person? Just look at their opposing counterpart: Spiritual Wickedness in High Places. What are they doing in high places? Don't forget the Church is supposed to be seated with Christ in "high places". For when Christ resurrected, He was seated in the "heavenly" or "high" places... (Ephesians 1:20). And God has made believers sit in the heavenly places in Christ Jesus. (Ephesians 2:6) Pictorially, believers' position in the heavenly places makes us luminaries to the world. (Matthew 5:14).

Now the work of the Spiritual Wickedness in High Places is to make believers lose their luminary nature and the work of Pastors and Teachers is to make believers maintain their luminary nature. None of the ministry gifts can mature believers like the Pastor/Teacher does. What happens, now that "prophets" are all heading congregations? We should be careful not to change God's strategic pattern.

Gifts of a Prophet

I have, on several occasions, heard people say, "This is the way I am, I cannot do anything about it". Most of the time they are talking about temperaments. Such people lock themselves in certain behavioral patterns. But a group of Christian psychologists has suggested that we see our temperamental traits as tendencies and not destinies. It means one can improve upon one's innate traits.

In a similar way, many believers lock themselves up when it comes to spiritual gifts. But God always provides guides that can be applied in many areas of our lives.

In Galatians 5:22, nine virtues are described as the fruit of the Spirit; not fruits. It simply means it is one virtue manifesting itself in nine different ways as the need arises. In other words, one cannot have love without having joy; and another cannot have joy without having peace etc. It means, potentially, all the nine-fold fruit of the spirit is resident in every believer but practically and experientially others are more present than others. The same principle applies to the gifts of the Spirit.

Many times we explain the gifts as if the Holy Spirit stands outside and throws in a gift or two and that is it. No. The Spirit indwells us with all His power. For practicality and order, different facets of the charismata manifest but by the SAME SPIRIT. So potentially, every believer is endowed with all that the Spirit distributes. Relatively then, each one of us is potentially endowed with all the nine gifts of the Spirit.

If anyone is sick and the regular brother with the gift of healing is not available, I should believe God and allow the Holy Spirit to manifest the gift of healing through me. So every believer can avail him or herself to prophesy, speak in tongues etc.; it is by the SAME Spirit. The same applies to the ministry gifts. One ministry gift is called a Teacher and yet one major qualification for every Christian leader is the ability to teach. (1Timothy 3:2) So within the Evangelist can be an apostolic potential.

In fact, at times some operating ministry gifts may start with other gifts before the main one comes up strong. For some reason, the apostolic gift does not always come up immediately. Many pastor and evangelize for years before the apostolic gift is finally crystallized. When the need arises, there is grace for us to be used in the prophetic and the miraculous. God can use the donkey; you over-qualify.

Gifts of a Prophet [2]

Let us create this scenario:

In a house, there is a tool room. There are tools for carpentry, farming, car maintenance, electrical and masonry. Interestingly, some of the tools for car maintenance are used to tighten the other tools. So one can be seen selecting car maintenance tools whilst the assignment that day could be farming or carpentry. There could also be carpentry work on the farm or mechanical work to service the harvester. So the selection of the tools in itself does not directly determine the assignment; it is the direction of the tool holder.

So one operating in the gifts of word of wisdom, word of knowledge and the gifts of prophecy and speaking in tongues does not necessarily make one a prophet. The gifts are a pool of equipment for service. In the early Church, a group of seven men were chosen to serve tables. The Bible makes it obvious that these seven men had access to the equipment room: *"Therefore, friends, select from among yourselves seven men of good standing, FULL of the SPIRIT and of wisdom, whom we may appoint to this task. (Acts 6:3).* And the passage following records those at the ministry gifts level saying, *"while we, for our part, will devote ourselves to prayer and to serving the word" (Acts 6:4).*

Unfortunately, today, there are men of God especially strong in prayer and others, in word delivery. However, that specialization is unfortunate; Light (the word) and heat (prayer) are of the same essence. So different spiritual assignments may need the same source of spiritual equipment.

The fact that prophets depend on the revelatory and utterance gifts does not necessarily mean anyone who operates them is a prophet. In fact, Paul told the members of the Corinthian church to covet to prophesy and forbid not to speak with tongues. So prophecy can be a congregational experience. (Acts 6:3).

Also, different gifts can yield the same results as long as we depend on the Holy Spirit. Some are in churches where there is no direct prophetic ministration but the faithful application of the word they are taught keep them victorious. In fact, the Spirit-inspired teaching of the word is the purest form of all ministrations.

The Resurrection and the Prophetic [1]

Luke 24:13-35: *And behold, two of them went that same day to a village called Emmaus... And it came to pass, that, while they communed and reasoned, Jesus Himself drew near, and went with them. But their eyes were holden ("blinded") that they should not know Him. And He said unto them, 'What manner of communications are these that ye (you) have with one another, as ye walk, and are sad? ...Cleopas, answering said...'Art thou only a stranger in Jerusalem? ... Concerning Jesus who was a PROPHET mighty in DEED and WORD...condemned to death... and... crucified ...today is the third day since these things were done...certain women... found not His body... saying He was alive. And certain of them which were with us...found it even so...Then He said unto them, 'O fools and slow of heart to believe... the prophets...'Ought not Christ to have suffered these things and to enter into His glory? 'And beginning at Moses and all the prophets, He expounded unto them all the scriptures concerning Himself...He made as though He would have gone further. But they constrained Him ...And He went in to tarry with them...as He sat at meat with them, He took bread and blessed it, and brake, and gave to them. And their eyes were opened, and they knew Him; And He vanished out of their sight. And they said one to another, did not our hearts burn within us, while he talked with us by the way, and while He opened to us the scriptures?"*

We have no better example when it comes to the prophetic than Jesus our Lord. Nicodemus describes him as a "Teacher come from God" because no man can do the miracles you do. (John 3:2) So in Jesus, Nicodemus puts the ministries of a Teacher and a miracle-worker together. It means those who operate in the miraculous must also give a high level attention to teaching the word of God.

After the resurrection, Our Lord Jesus personally joins two disciples on their way to a village called Emmaus. That was a miracle enough but their eyes were closed from identifying Him. A miracle in itself may not open our eyes to God. The wilderness Israel saw miracles upon miracles right from Egypt through their forty-year journey but they were among the most hard-hearted of God's people. These disciples knew Christ as a PROPHET, mighty in DEED and WORD, just as Nicodemus described Him. However, they were still lost as to Christ's power to resurrect. Why? According to Jesus, they had not taken the scriptures seriously. *'Oh fools and slow of heart to believe all that the prophets (the Old Testament) have spoken: And beginning from Moses and all the prophets, he expounded unto them in all the scriptures the things concerning Himself.' (Luke 24:25, 26).*

Here is a Prophet mighty in deed, using the WORD to reveal Himself. Miracles are powerful but the WORD is UNCOMPARABLE. The conversation was getting interesting so they cordially restrained Jesus from going further. They now have heard His voice and they opened the door. (Revelation 3:20) He came in and supped (ate) with them. Immediately their eyes opened to see who He is, He immediately vanished.

"They said to each other, 'Were not our hearts burning within us while He was talking to us on the road? WHILE HE WAS OPENING THE SCRIPTURES TO US?'

The WORD will set your heart ablaze. Yes, there will always be intermittent miraculous manifestations of the resurrected Christ but the PRIMARY way of revealing Himself to us is through His WORD in our HEARTS.

The Resurrection and the Prophetic [2]

John 20:19-29: *So when it was evening on ...the first day of the week, when the doors were shut where the disciples were, for fear of the Jews, Jesus came and stood in their mist and said unto them 'Peace be unto you'...He showed them both His hands and His side. The disciples rejoiced when they saw the Lord. So Jesus said to them...As the Father has sent Me, I also send you. And when He had said this, He breathed on them and said to them, 'Receive the Holy Spirit. If you forgive the sins of any, their sins have been forgiven them; if you retain the sins of any, they have been retained. But*

Thomas, one of the twelve, called Didymus, was not with them when Jesus came. So the other disciples were saying to him, 'We have seen the Lord!' But he said unto them, 'Unless I see in His hands the imprint of the nails, and put my finger into the place of the nails, and put my hand into His side, I will not believe. After eight days His disciples were again inside, and Thomas with them. Jesus came, the doors having been shut, and stood in their mist and said, 'Peace be with you'. Then He said to Thomas, 'Reach here with your finger, and see My hands; and reach here your hand and put it into My side; and do not be unbelieving, but believing.' Thomas answered and said to Him, My Lord and my God. Jesus said to Him, 'Because you have seen Me, have you believed? BLESSED ARE THEY WHO DID NOT SEE, AND YET BELIEVE."

Just as it was with the two disciples on their way to Emmaus, the resurrection opened the disciples up into some spiritual dimensions; seeing our Lord enter with doors tightly closed. Our Lord's first spiritual blessing was that of peace. Peace be unto you. Revelation of the supernatural should introduce peace instead of fear; a divine commission instead of self-propagation (as My Father has sent me...) and the Holy Spirit as the believer's breath (way of life). He also emphasized the subject of forgiveness. Jesus had forgiven those who tortured Him whilst in pain but in His resurrection and victory, he still introduces the subject of forgiveness.

What do you do with spiritual power? Do issues of Peace and forgiveness come up? Amazingly, Thomas is missing at this divine fellowship. When he was later told, his response was that he WILL not believe without empirical evidence. He did not say he COULD not believe. Faith, though a gift from God, is a moral decision. A known apologist convinced an atheist that God is real. After, he asked him if he was ready to commit his life to Christ. His response was in the negative; he was not ready to pay the price. It is not automatic that people will believe if they saw Jesus physically. Otherwise why did many of the Pharisees remain stiff-necked after seeing His miracles and His resurrection? And if notable divine revelations cannot guarantee faith, what do some want to achieve with the fake and the exaggerations? Miracles stir faith but it is only the Word of God that sustains it. Faith comes by...the Word of God. (Romans 10:17).

Jesus appears again. This time Thomas was there. He gets the opportunity to see and touch the resurrected Lord. He now believes and makes a solid declaration of faith- MY LORD AND MY GOD. But to Jesus, the declaration has come quite late. "Blessed are they who did not see, and yet believe".

You are blessed if you believe in Heaven without having a vision about it. You are blessed if you believe in victory when you do not have a prophet to show you who your exact enemies are. I know you admire those whose spiritual eyes are opened as soon as they close the physical ones. You are also blessed by your daily dependence on the Word of God.

The Resurrection and the Prophetic [3]

Acts 9:1-16: *"Now Saul, still breathing threats and murder against the disciples of the Lord, went to the High Priest, and asked for letters from him to the synagogues of Damascus, so that if he found any belonging to the Way, both men and women, he might bring them bound to Jerusalem. As he was...approaching Damascus...suddenly a light from Heaven flashed around him; and he fell to the ground and heard a voice saying to him, 'Saul, Saul, why are you persecuting me?"And he said, 'Who are you Lord?' And He said, I am Jesus whom you are persecuting but get up and enter the city, and it will be told you what you must do...They brought him into Damascus. And he was three days without sight, and neither ate nor drank. Now there was a disciple at Damascus named Ananias; and the Lord said to him in a vision, 'Ananias.' And he said, Here I am Lord. 'And the Lord said to him, get up and go to the street called Straight, and inquire at the house of Judah for a man from Tarsus named Saul, for he is praying, and he has seen in a vision a man named Ananias come in and lay his hands on him, so that he might regain his sight.'*

But Ananias answered, 'Lord, I have heard from many about this man, how much harm he did to your saints at Jerusalem; and here he has authority from the chief priests to bind all who call on your name.'

But the Lord said to him, 'Go for he is a chosen instrument of Mine to bear My name before the gentiles and kings and the sons of Israel; for I will show him how much he must suffer for My name's sake'.

It is amazing the extent to which religious or doctrinal misunderstandings can go. In this passage the way of Christ, the only way of salvation was branded a heresy. We all must be careful of a blanket branding of the apparent controversial prophetic ministry today. Every fake has its genuine. Let us be careful because in an attempt to cut down the tares, we may also cut down the wheat. (Matthew 13:25-30). The best we can do is to out plant the tares with more wheat. We need to dare do programs that will correct the damage. We should support ministers staying faithful to the Word.

The caution is that every attack on a believer is an attack on our Lord Jesus Himself. That was what Christ told Paul; "Why are you persecuting me?" The assurance though is that God is more concerned about the mess today than ourselves. With the situation in this passage He came down miraculously to intervene. What a day of joy when a dreaded persecutor enters the home of his intended victims blind and helpless. He is with us and He is Lord. What the Lord was demanding in all these was submission. Paul had to submit his will to Christ by obeying Him to seek help from the people he was going to harm. Ananias was not comfortable ministering to Saul but as soon as our Lord told him, "I have chosen him", he had to put his reservations aside and say, "Yes Lord"

It is the Lord. So then neither is he that planteth (plants) anything, neither he that watereth (waters); but God that giveth (gives) increase. (1Corinthians 3:7) We must submit to the purposes of God. Prophetically Paul had a more dramatic experience than Ananias. But Paul's experience was a confrontation whilst Ananias' was a communication. Paul's more dramatic experience left him physically blind and Ananias' less dramatic experience left him with the grace to heal and to restore. The one with the more dramatic experience needed prayer from the one with the less dramatic one. Whatever be our experience let us be humble. It is amazing why God did not give the most important instructions to Paul in that dramatic encounter but asked him to go to the believers in Damascus to be told what to do. No prophetic experience is bigger than the Church and no experience is bigger than the need to be discipled. Be humble.

The Prophetic and the Preaching of the Word

Prophecy can be summarized as God's means of communicating to man. That is why at some biblical instances prophecy simply means preaching. The preaching aspect of prophecy is termed forth-telling whilst the prediction aspect is called foretelling. However, church tradition has, over the years, skinned the preaching aspect of prophecy away so the general definition of prophecy is strictly limited to prediction. Many preachers today, to some extent, pass for an Old Testament prophet. However, because of the traditional interpretation of prophecy, many dynamic men of God have been disqualified from possessing any prophetic instincts.

And a selective aspect has hijacked the office and the title. And interestingly, this selective aspect has pruned off other necessary branches of ministry like the preaching and the teaching of God's word and limited themselves only to the traditional form of prophecy. Many have denied themselves the other necessary and beautiful forms of ministry as stated earlier and engrafted the "prophetic" into the stumps of all the cut-off branches. So to many of the men of God, it is impossible not to prophesy all the time because that is the only ministry they have remaining. So where a scriptural guideline could have been effective, the "prophetic" becomes the only available "solution"; even when the grace to prophesy does not seem to be present.

At such times some "prophets" create scenarios that will extract "a prophetic solution" from the seeker. All the probabilities are worked out. At other times the history goes beyond one's age of consciousness so the seeker does not have the ability to confirm or deny. On other occasions there is indeed a prophetic diagnosis but a solid scriptural prescription is not available. In fact, some seekers are rather drawn away from their Bibles and instead canonize the directions of the "prophet".

What did you bring from the Consultation?

Jesus always ministered to the multitudes. But it is obvious that the multitudes were at the lower end of the ladder of his audience. He could not also trust the multitudes with the meat of His teachings. It was also obvious at His crucifixion that the bulk of the multitudes could not be transformed into disciples. By the Ascension five hundred disciples had seen Him but by Pentecost, only ten days after ascension, only about one hundred and twenty were Holy-Spirit-worthy.

At the teaching on the bread of life in John chapter six, the multitudes had to desert Christ because they could not comprehend the thrust of His message. Why didn't the disciples also desert him? What the disciples perceived as the words of life, the multitudes had labeled a taboo.

Teaching is at its best when the number of the audience is relatively smaller. The quality is better when shared among a few than when the multitudes scramble. So in Matthew chapter five, the Rabbi had seen the multitudes but the teaching for the day belonged to the disciples who were, on other occasions, not different from the multitudes anyway. But of course the better of the two. Evidently, the disciples were a better 'gamble' than the multitudes. Having distanced Himself from the multitudes into the mountains, his disciples came unto Him.

He knew that the multitudes followed Him for a purpose - TO BE BLESSED. However, He knew the multitudes were not ready for this type of blessings He was going to introduce. In John chapter 6, the people wanted to make Jesus a King because He gave them bread. But on a day He taught, the people, who had come to enthrone Him, immediately deserted Him. Amazingly when many Christians talk about blessing, it is mostly about filling the stomach only. Many are not interested about feeding their mind so as to improve their hearts. So Jesus separates His disciples from the multitudes and starts to teach them about the highest forms of blessing outlined in Matthew 5:1-12;

Spiritual poverty; spiritual mourning; spiritual meekness; spiritual hunger and thirst; merciful to others; purity of heart; peacemaking; and righteousness-induced persecution. Why are these the highest forms of blessing? Because of the results they bring.

They lead to:

Possessing of the Kingdom; enjoying God's comfort; inheriting the Kingdom's earth; spiritual fullness; positioned to receive mercy; a deeper relationship with God; being noticed as a child of God; and an awaiting reward in Heaven. Interestingly Jesus links these spiritual attitudes to the way of life of the prophets of old, in Matthew 5:12. In other words, these attitudes can reflect the way of life of a prophet.

Just as Jesus did in Matthew chapter 5, today's prophet, because pursued by many, has introduced a way for a more targeted and therefore a quality ministration called consultation. At this consultation, ministry is more personalized. My question to all beneficiaries of such consultations is: "Are you anywhere near Matthew chapter 5 when you exited the consultation room?"

1. Has your attitude become like that of the sincere needy?

2. Have you become repentant?

3. What has happened to submission?

4. What has become your utmost desire?

5. How do you treat others?

6. Did you see God during and after the consultation?

7. Has the consultation improved your relations or hardened the hatred you harbored?

8. What did the prophet say he was going to do to those who persecuted you?

The Miracle you have been searching for

Christians move from one man of God to another because they believe they have needs that only a miracle can meet. Many Christians seek God for a special breakthrough. The poor want a relief and the rich may want protection from drawers-back. The question therefore is what is a miracle? A miracle happens when divinity intervenes in the natural way things happen. When that happens we say it is supernatural; it means it is above what we are used to. It beats imagination. The Bible makes it plain that everything seen came from the unseen. (Hebrews 11:3). This confirms the fact that the spiritual is the source of the seen. The physical therefore is not independent of the spiritual and many times, the unlimited spiritual comes to strengthen and empower the physical. This phenomenon gives birth to concepts such as anointing. This is when God empowers mortal man with extra-terrestrial powers to perform what was otherwise impossible.

It is important to state that spiritual or the supernatural is very respectful of the physical or the natural. So when the supernatural intervenes into the physical it consummates into the physical.

Christ, the Son of God, is God, but when He incarnated into humanity, He took upon Himself the form of a man. (Philippians 2:1). So many miracles consummate into the physical that we many times overlook their miraculous origin. Since the creation of the universe the Sun every day 'rises' from the East and 'sets' at the West. Any time there is a slight change in the routine, the whole world is attracted to it. It is interesting to note that when testimonies are called for at Church, it is only those who have had a negative adjustment in their lives and restored to the normal that consider themselves fortunate to have a testimony. Those who have been fortunate enough not to have had any negative alterations in their lives do not consider themselves recipients of a mighty miracle. So many move from place to place with this mindset of seeking for miracles that already exist in another form. This is one reason many Christians remain unthankful. Somebody have all the money you are seeking for but spends a bulk searching for the health you have but not appreciating God for.

Your childless marriage, though very unfortunate, is so peaceful; that fruitful couple has all their children on drugs. Even we pastors whom you come to seek blessings from, have our own issues. So you see, God has not abandoned you. Just like spiritual gifts, our miracles vary from person to person. Similarly, our battles differ from person to person. One thing, I believe, that provides the keys of victory in our battles is identifying our already existing miracles and appreciating God for them. Not doing so denies us the faith we need to be victorious in our battles and we are left with that desperation that opens the door for manipulation and abuse.

Yes, it is not as simple as narrated; I agree. Some of the battles others go through are fierce. The question then is, "What is the reason for all these battles?" The enemy has seen something in you that you are yet to see yourself. We are created with the capacity to receive miracles that come to us in many forms. (Isaiah 8:18) I believe it is easier to receive a miracle than to manage it. I also believe a miracle has a longer time span and a broader purpose than many experience. One miracle is capable of 'sustaining us through life. Solomon's request for wisdom brought him prosperity and long life (1Kings 3:-11).

The prophet's widow had her oil multiplied; the sons were redeemed and they lived on the rest. (2Kings 4:1-7) Elijah's angelic food sustained him for a forty-day journey to God's presence (1Kings 19:1-8). Can it be that you have already received that one miracle you will ever need in your life? Can it be that this miracle has strengthened your faith to personally fight every battle that confronts you in this life? Maybe you already have it; Settle, confront your challenges on your knees and cut short your roaming whilst the 'weaker ones' continue to seek help.

The Cycle of the Prophetic Encounter

Jesus therefore being weary from his journey was sitting thus by the well. It was about the sixth hour (about noon). There came a woman of Samaria to draw water. Jesus said to her, "give me a drink". the Samaritan woman therefore said to him, "how is it that you being a Jew, ask me for a drink since I am a Samaritan woman?"... Jesus answered and said to her "If you knew the gift of God, and who it is who says to you, "Give me a drink", you would have asked Him and He would have given you living water"....Jesus answered and said to her "Everyone who drinks of this water shall thirst again but whoever drinks of the water that I shall give him will never thirst, but the water that I shall give him shall become in him a well of water springing up to eternal life".

The woman said to Him, "Sir, give me this water, so I will not be thirsty, nor come all the way here to draw". He said to her, "Go call your husband, and come here". The woman answered and said, "I have no husband." Jesus said to her, "You have well said, "I have no husband"; for you have had five husbands and one whom you now have is not your husband; this you have said truly". The woman said to Him," Sir, I perceive that you are a prophet ... I know that Messiah is coming... when that One comes, He will declare all things to us." Jesus said to her, "I who speaks to you I am He". So the woman left the water pot, and went into the city, and said to the men "Come see a man who told me all things that I have done; this is not the Christ, is it?" They went out of the city and were coming to Him. And from that city many of the Samaritans believed in Him because of the word of the woman who testified, "He told me all the things that I have done". And they were saying to the woman, "It is no longer because of what you said that we believe, for we have heard for ourselves and know that this One is indeed the Savior of the world". (John 4:6-42).

The prophetic encounter has been so much re-structured to the extent that the human element involved today far outweighs its core elements. What is this that I am hearing that many of these 'encounters' are even staged. It is obvious that many of the biblically-recorded prophetic encounters started from 'unrelated' settings. Moses was on his routine shepherds task (Exodus 3:1-5). Paul was on his way to imprison believers (Acts 9:1-6). King Saul was searching for his lost sheep (1Samuel 9:3-27).

In our passage, the Samaritan woman was nowhere near religion when she had this prophetic encounter with our Lord. It was not only the Samaritan woman who was nowhere near a divine encounter, but our Lord Himself wore an apparent weariness that may have disguised Him from a One to give eternal life. His hair probably looked unkempt and His body sweaty.

The situation looked so unpredictable that the woman only saw a Jew. The interactive language was so unreligious that the woman literally was not ready to offer our Lord Jesus any 'assistance'. The purity of the prophetic is based in its originality; no gimmicks. The encounters sampled above did not expect any prophetic encounter, neither had they requested for it. They were not at a prophetic gathering. There was not a demand for it.

However the content of the encounter between the Samaritan woman and Christ was so scripturally-based and centered on the theme of eternal life. Jesus' approach was so unconventional and yet, in no time, His identity as a "Prophet" had been disclosed. Though Jesus knew everything about this woman, He allowed her to personally open up simply by asking her to bring her husband.

In that case she was her own prophetess first. Jesus' approach allowed her to name her own situation. Jesus gave her the 'credit' for the revelation; "You have truly said, I don't have a husband." Not only is it interactive to be our own first prophets but many must learn to have sound and biblical prophetic priorities. I am sure many leave the prophetic grounds surprised. They may be excited about the prophetic directions but some may wonder about the 'selectivity' of the revelations.

A taxi driver once told me he played along a prophetic ministration. The 'prophet' had told him he (the taxi driver) had purchased a land and he deceptively affirmed. He confessed to me that he does not even know the price of a piece of land. He also confessed to me about his infidelity in marriage and he was surprised, that his infidelity (his truest state) did not come up in the prophetic revelation and besides what came up was nowhere near the truth. Most recorded divine encounters do not end without revealing the holiness of God and the sinfulness of man. The prophet Isaiah said *"woe is me, for I am a man of unclean lips" (Isaiah 6:5)*. After Peter realized he had seen the resurrected Lord, he jumped into the sea because was 'naked' (John 21:7). Moses was commanded to remove his shoes because where he had the encounter was a holy ground (Exodus 3:5). The woman caught in adultery, though shown mercy was commanded to go and sin no more. (John 8:11).

I agree people should not be 'embarrassed' by exposing their struggles with sin but encounters that are divine should carry a certain sanctimonious presence that causes one to see the need to totally surrender to God. However I have been surprised, that this is not the direction most of prophetic encounters today are towing.

The Samaritan woman's encounter was a spiritual ladder; it was a climbing experience. It started with Jesus being described as a Jew, it climbed to identifying our Lord as a prophet. In no time, the conversation now centers on the Messiah. What happened to spiritual hunger for God and righteousness? Are our prophetic encounters getting scripturally and spiritually deeper? Or it will continue to remain at the descriptions of the details of one's room. No wonder the need to sit behind one's Bible for hours and days to do a detailed Bible studies is becoming a thing of the past. If the man of God can reveal a couple of details about a person, ministry is accomplished; hands are clapped and exhaustive teachings of God's word may no more be necessary.

The climax of every encounter must be a conviction. It must be a conviction that is worth the sacrifice of everything. "Then answered Peter and said unto Him, Behold, we have forsaken all, and followed Thee; what shall we have therefore?" (Matthew 19:27). The Samaritan woman left her water pot behind, went to the city to broadcast the encounter. She gave up her need for physical water and considered the need of others for the living water. "The whole city must hear this", she may have said this to herself. Following her, the whole city did. They had believed the testimony of her spiritual encounter. (John 4:39) But this testimony did not necessarily call for another miracle; they needed to hear His word and they did. Because of His words, many more became believer's" (4:41).

They said to the woman, "We no longer believe just because of what you said; now we have heard for ourselves, and we know that this Man is really the Savior of the world. Salvation of souls must be the end of every prophetic encounter.

Be Blessed Amen